Touri

FOR AMANDA

Acknowledgements

Grateful acknowledgement is due to the editors of the following periodicals, where some of these poems have appeared: *The Critical Quarterly*, *Green River Review* (USA), *Pacific Quarterly* (NZ), *PN Review*, *Poetry Durham*, *Temenos* and *The Times Literary Supplement*.

The poems in section III appeared (some in earlier versions) in *Fools' Paradise* (Carcanet New Press, 1977).

"The Legacy: Emmer Green, 1956" is a fictional elaboration of an incident mentioned in *Wilfred Owen: Collected Letters*, ed. Harold Owen and John Bell, London (Oxford University Press), 1967, p.1.

Vignettes XXI incorporates a number of phrases from Bewick's autobiographical memoir: see *A Memoir of Thomas Bewick*, ed. Iain Bain, London (Oxford University Press), 1975.

First published in 1987 by
CARCANET PRESS LIMITED
208-212 Corn Exchange, Manchester M4 3BQ
and
198 Sixth Avenue, New York, NY 10013

All rights reserved.

Copyright © Grevel Lindop 1987

British Library Cataloguing in Publication Data

Lindop, Grevel
   Tourists.
   I. Title
   821'.914   PR6062.I475

ISBN 0-85635-697-2

The publisher acknowledges financial assistance from
the Arts Council of Great Britain.

Typeset in 10pt Palatino by Bryan Williamson, Manchester
Printed in England by SRP Ltd, Exeter

Contents

I

To Scheherazade	9
White Horse	10
The Legacy: Emmer Green, 1956	11
My Grandmother's Opal	12
O.S. Sheet 117: Chester	13
Mappa Mundi	14
The Key	15
A Welsh Farm	16
Pennine Way	17
On White Moss	18
Harvest	21
Dark	22
The Suppliants	23
In Quintum Novembris	24
Latoun	25
On Helm Crag	26
The Traveller at Yazd	27
The Chinese Temple in Hollywood Road, Hong Kong	28
In Europe Everything Has Been Painted	29
Summer Pudding	30
Migraine	32
Snow	33
Russet Apples	34
Fidelities	35
Signal	38
Little Girl on the Lawn	39
Leaf Wading	40
"Look"	41
Monuments	42
Lamp and Bright Page	46

II

Vignettes: Poems for Twenty-One Wood Engravings by Thomas Bewick	49

III

The Barrel-Dance	73
Caption	74
Buying Valentines	75

Dictionary	76
Ovid in Exile	77
Winter Poem for Osip Mandelstam	78
Ampersand	79
Mirror and Candle	80
The Hands	81
The Tattooist	82
Bluebeard's Wife	83
The Tell-Tale Heart	84
The Core	85
Shropshire Union Canal	85

IV

Tourists	87

I

To Scheherazade

Your unperturbed voice
with a serenely repeated movement
like the scimitar-stroke
of a great bird's wing, lays open
a rift of clear air
through our silence, a coloured swathe
engrossed with human action:
debate, betrayal, ruse, justice.

Through the page as through a pane
we look out on a spacious real world
where people say "But Allah alone is wise..."
finding a baboon an artist in calligraphy
or the lost ring in the belly of a fish.

In that saying, the imperturbable
perspective: they are real
to themselves in the same way
as to us. In that, and the knowledge
(on which especially your love is founded)
that there is a story opening
inside every other story,
and that of these it is given us to know
an infinite number, but still less than all.

White Horse

1940: a summer of mythical heat,
and up on the Berkshire Downs my father in khaki
with an OCTU contingent spread out over the hillside
spading slabs of turf from the back of a lorry

to bury the White Horse. Square by square
the turf is laid and the blinding chalk goes under
the rough green skin of the down, secure
from the moon's betrayal and the jealous bomber.

When landmarks were allowed again, someone else
dug it up: perhaps he would have liked a share
in that restorative work, but had no chance
to turn his hand to it. And how much more

of England, of us, stayed buried after
those years, those wars? Whatever is concealed
may be forgotten – the moment of doubt, the toy soldier,
the gold collar sunk in the stubborn field.

Protecting ourselves, it's ourselves we bury
and with time the ploughshares of habit go over
until the desire or the thing unspoken seem ordinary
dullness lodged in stony ground. Father,

let us uncover the white horse of love,
delicate as a bone brooch, solid as the chalk
heart of the down, the ground on which we move,
undiminished, cut free and living into the rock.

The Legacy: Emmer Green, 1956

Let the boy try. The chisel's edge is slid
into the crack. A few businesslike knocks
should do it. Gently now. The blistered lid
resists, resists. He levers at the box,

I hold it steady. (All day long they've worked
to sort Miss Mary's things. A magpie-nest
of clothes, toys, jewellery, papers, bills, that lurked
in bags, chests, cupboards, clocks; and with the rest,

I'm told, the poet's letters, stuffed in absurd
odd corners. They asked *us* to have a go
at these old trunks and crates. Why she left word
the Scouts should open this, I'll never know.)

A splintering crack. It gives. A musty cover
of cloth, and under it the dull green
nubbed bulk of a fully-loaded revolver.
Army issue. Nineteen-seventeen.

Thirty corroded live rounds in a pouch
of mouldy leather. Gasping, the lads crowd in.
Treasure-trove! No. No: better not touch.
Steadying my hands, I pack the things again.

In mildewed lint and sour buttery tarnish
the huge unwieldy ghost of war is laid.
My fingers nearly slip on the dull varnish.
Lifting the box, I learn that I'm afraid.

My Grandmother's Opal

Nowadays I can find no picture of her.
I lost the only photograph I had
moving house; nothing else came to me,
so all I keep now is this opulent bead,

milky violet, craggy sugar-white
and crumpled goldleaf fused into the one
hurtfully alluring crystal depth
of opal, her favourite stone,

which like a scrying-globe entraps the eye;
though I should need more than a jeweller's glass
to see what figures might flaw the blue mist
or walk unscathed out of that golden furnace,

distant and enigmatic, bright and small
as now my memories of her: some stories
and nonsense-rhymes she riddled me out of her childhood,
odd scents she used, her sharp, affectionate gaze,

skirts I buried my face in, and the love
which like an animal I could discern,
inhabit like warmth but never comprehend
or, so young I was, return.

So here it is, my grandmother's opal,
centrepiece of a necklace broken and strewn
who now knows where? And of no use to me,
too large for a ring, too splendid to cut down,

message I can't read, riches not mine
to spend or give, unexplained trust I hold.
I keep it: but where shall I set it, this one spark
saved from the fiery heart of a lost world?

O.S. Sheet 117: Chester

Spreading it, I uncrease a map of childhood
Sundays: Peckforton Hills' huddle of greenwood
From which the Castle jutted like a toy fort,
Suiting its name; Farndon, where I caught
Eels that thrashed on the grass to inextricable
Furious snarls of fishing-line, seamless muscle,
Red clay and tangy slime that stuck to my fingers –
Odourless now, and tracing Dee's meanders
Through pale fretwork of villages on squared paper,
The land ruled flat and stretched as compromise
Through memory's declivities and spires.
   Kinnerton, where my father's fathers farmed;
The Parks with its hayfields, where one sunwarmed
Afternoon between wars my father was photographed,
Boy in a school cap, perched on the iron seat
Of a horsedrawn reaper, where fields are reaped still,
Though nearer Wrexham now. And Bickerton Hill
To the north, where it seemed the sun always shone
So hot the hazels, sand, bracken-fronds
Glowed like copper in the wavy air
And I imagined the sun dug himself in there
At nights like a fiery hedgehog under the drifts
Of brown oakleaves and gnarled, furry fernroots,
Below the scorched hill making his restless bed.
   Places I may dream of when I'm dead,
Though glimpsed just long enough to wake the blood
With tremor of things hardly understood.
Above them, Beeston Castle on its outcrop
Of battered sandstone and, shown on no map,
The caves beneath, whose globed chambers, scooped
As if with a spoon from the honey-coloured rock,
Led from cavern to cavern, colder and further
Into the hill, where I ventured with my brother
On the damp sand floor to find the end, almost
Until daylight from the cave mouth was lost –
Almost – but could not quite bear to break
That last frail thread of light, would turn and race back
To the opening, and then again trek inwards,
Fronting the unmapped depth, hearing our shouts
Echo down into the darkness, where
We longed to follow them and wouldn't dare.

Mappa Mundi

The thirteenth-century world-map in Hereford Cathedral

for Neil Colyer

Shaped like a spread cloak, as Strabo
would have said, or for us like an envelope
with the flap up, this trimmed squareyard
of sheepskin nailed to its wooden stretcher
is space for a round world of ragged
continents, ocean-rimmed, mermaid-hymned, spoked
with a cross of seas, pivoting like a wheel
on Jerusalem, nave of creation.

Here are Babel and Rome,
the Strait of Gibraltar and the Earthly Paradise
on its island out at the sun's East Gate
with a wall of fire to deter trespassers
like us; Ararat, where in clear weather the Ark
may be seen by the sharpeyed, timbers firmly stove
on the first mountain-tip given up
by the Flood; the cannibal Essedones, and here
dogheaded Lapps, the crocodile and centaur.

Here is a mirror, and the world inside it
no stranger than your eyes, the palm
of your hand or your stressed heart bound
by its rivers of blood, home of boredom and madness,
the journey in the body's battered coracle
towards the imagined garden. Think kindly,
then, of Richard the Clerk, who dared place
his own Clee Hill in this corner, not so far
from Jerusalem but a man might hope to walk there
once in a lifetime, covering the earth
with no finer vellum than the soles of pilgrim feet.

The Key

Samuel Palmer sketched the hill
I climb to reach my house tonight:
the moon's a coin rubbed thin with use
wrapped in torn clouds, and up ahead
the wet road gleams with black and white.

The farm gate creaks, the farmdogs bark,
their cry torn upwards on the wind
and on the wind receding now
as five years' distance falls between
that night and this reluctant mind

that will not let the past be past
but haunts a place that cannot be
again, and like a ghost would peer
in at the glass to find myself.
I grope in memory for the key:

a door once shut is always shut,
the reader there by gaslight died
five years ago, and here I am.
The wind has torn the house away,
time and the rain have stepped inside.

The mind tugs at its guyrope yet,
as if that place were not secure
from all the winds of hope and loss;
as if the key would not dissolve
always before I reach that door.

A Welsh Farm

The lane ends; and the eye sorts out
among the jigsaw-shapes of trees
bits of a house: two walls upright,
a crushed concertina of stairs

over a floor scaly with dropped
slates, and a window in its frame, whole
but white with web and lichen, propped
by nettles since the kitchen fell.

Floorboards of an upper room
slope down at forty-five degrees
to mounds of rotten lath and lime
sunk in bramble and goosegrass,

and at the top where boards meet plaster
the rusty head and foot of an iron
bedstead perch, carelessly placed there
when someone left, still clinging on,

absurd, among the leaves and wind.
How could that sleeper ever dream
his bed would outlast all he owned?
And now its ends so clearly seem

two brackets closing up a life.
I walk back through the dripping trees
uneasy, compromised, as if
I were the puzzle's missing piece

and had myself dreamed of all this
between that black foot and black head,
though my shoes seem to tread real grass
and leave impression on the mud

until the wind wakes up and starts
threshing the trodden earth with rain,
still driving men and farms and fields
by inches to their dissolution.

Pennine Way

Midway we stop to hitch a gate, then stand
letting the landscape settle into place
below us: meshed in trees, the castle's mound
and cube of fretted stone; tussocked grass

that falls away and softens as it falls
to distant minor pastoral; a scoop
of glacial valley netted with slate walls;
impossible green fields dotted with sheep;

Great Hartside shoving through its wrap of fir
below the blue diminished peaks that shelve
out towards Hawbeck, lost within the air,
raindrift and sunhaze, while the clouds evolve

a single moment in the slow creation
of all the spectrum spread from rock to light,
from light to mind, from thought back to the lichen
you finger on the top bar of the gate.

Significant and baffling as a life,
it focuses our silence. If we talk
the meaning all around us spills, as if
our truest word were holding all words back –

which may be true. Years of dead angers like
those slate-tips piled above Greensaddle hang
a heritage, a threat, a useless black
step-pyramid, a pressure on the tongue.

We cannot talk. And so we walk instead,
and where a stream breaks into spray on stone
we lean against a bridge's parapet
to watch rock-shattered water vanish down

among the leaves. We stand so long it might
(I tell myself) even be true that each
had felt a wish grow in his silent heart
and prayed the vocal stream to lend us speech.

On White Moss

in memory of Pete Laver (1947-83)

I climb the path again,
wet clay and mud into air
sweet with must of blackberries and sodden
bracken the year lays down
as I would lay what brings me here –
question, aesthetic, love, or fear
of what might be forgotten,
or of too much remembering –
into the making of another year.

A summit grows ahead,
and then another on its back
but there's no highest point
among the shattered cubes of rock,
wet peat and heather where the tracks are lost,
all shape an accident
of weather, time, the light
cutting memory at a certain angle,
a few words from a broken conversation.

Torn edge of cloud like blotting-paper soaks
colour from the skyline. North,
the roofs and smoke of Grasmere
are huddling in, faceless
for winter. Under my left hand,
south beyond the gulf of trees,
Rydal Water like a dropped
glass jigsaw-piece glints at the sky. I stand
against a hesitant, persistent wind.

What happened to our confidence
that meaning underlay all this,
or was all this? While we walked here we talked
of Ruskin and his peacock-feather,
and of the cave Coleridge found
below Nab Scar: you planned
to follow all the hints he left
in some notebook, trace back his steps
and reach that fable underneath the ground

no-one now will touch. But there you are,
hunched shoulders, toes kicking the stones,
your frown
searching the horizon for the next
sharpedged distinction or joke,
or swinging on a dead branch till it cracks
and we can drag it down, snagging and
thudding, through the trees,
then break it up to feed the cottage fire.

Only imagination loves the past
or warms its hands at those dry branches
now, so many days
of smoke have blown across
already. Passing your house
today, I found the iron gate
shut on your view of Silver How:
sweet smoke hung in the air,
someone else's cat strolled out and stared.

Everyone's a stranger. In the end
we live in one another's
thoughts: and though you move
again, I think, somewhere in the maze
of being, I can only
read you here, written into the book
of the landscape: which perhaps
is how you wanted it. When we last met
you told me of the time you walked up here

in spring, in morning, looking down
those rocks, and glimpsed a bright flutter like fire
caught in a crevice: wild azalea,
seeded from someone's garden. And I thought
of coming back another spring
to find it. Now October
wears out, and the trees
with their too-literal mourning
wait for the wind to tear their colours down.

It's time to go. Nothing's complete, a life
breaks down to fragments, the high
or low places of being. Children grow,
poems are read or forgotten,
whatever we gave someone takes.
I take your footholds down, seeing
a tract of sky that clears, rock-fragments shining
in the wet light; and one azalea,
burning and burning as the stars come out.

Harvest

Harvest passes these suburbs without a sign
Except the apples, cheaper in the shops;
But when I lift some flagstones a harvestman
Swings out from a crevice between two slabs –
Body brown and plump as a barleycorn –
And goes with lurching gait over the concrete,
No spider, but himself a walking web,
Feeling his way with all eight legs at once.

Twilight mellows towards dark, then hovers
Over what's visible. The stones resonate
Mildly to some light after the sun's.
I bed the last slab, straighten up to dust,
Gingerly, sand and soil from buzzing hands
And face to face meet a harvest moon
Floating remarkable over the trees,
Sharp as a blade, ripe as an apricot.

Harvestman, harvest moon – the words are blown
Here on a drift of language like husks
From seed long scattered. Walking back to the house,
I think of harvesters who worked these nights:
The swaying reaper three-legg'd with his scythe,
Binder and gleaner wakeful with the threat
Of rain, forearmed against impending winter,
Taking these extra hours of the moon's bounty –

Wading thighdeep among the silver grain
All those strange centuries before the streets
And patterned gardens were laid out like flags –
Cloud of lupin, gaudy slash of willowherb,
Laburnum powdering the usual pavement –
Their sweet pall drawn over these temperate fields
Where corn once grew, as it may grow again.

Dark

This is the first house where I've liked the dark.
Once night was void where backward things might lurk:
a burnt-out bulb or faulty switch meant fear,
lack of willed light the prelude to nightmare.

Not now. Closing curtains against the moon
I'm amused by how darkness closes in
reminding my hands of distance between doors,
my feet of soft carpets and counted stairs.

Is it that all ghosts have been stripped away
with the old paint and paper? Or that in me
some hidden hate has cooled and ceased to rebel?
I rejoice in the change but cannot tell.

I and the house are one. We settle down,
welcome rainfall and woodcreak. Let the night run,
let the mind's eye whose pleasure is to keep
dark in the dark mirror dreamless sleep.

The Suppliants

Poorer than the snail,
they hump no house on back but come
to beg though they don't know it, forming
no intention, drawn by aura of tealeaf
maybe, or spilled drop of milk
flavouring the air that threads
the crack at corner of my kitchen door.

Little-finger-sized,
two slugs without a thing to recommend them,
mere trust is all they have. They don't know I'm here
though they may feel the kitchen light
blink on or darkness plunge if I stand over them.
They don't ask for what they take,
nor could they reproach me if I killed them –

which I'd be ashamed
to do. I even wish them well,
whatever well for them may be. By dawn
they'll be gone; and if I put them out at night
they don't come back, their habits cryptic
as the tracks they leave, which answer to the moon
like veins of bright metal in the stone doorstep.

In Quintum Novembris

Summer has come to this:
a gambler's funeral.
Though you walk on wet gold
it is only that the trees have thrown in their hand,
the wind will sweep the board.
The spendthrift god lies cold.

His children have begged for pennies:
sulphur, saltpetre, charred wood
scent the approaching dark.
The sun toils in the mines of Scorpio.
Rockets assail an empty sky
and, flickering, fall back.

Latoun

Latoun, as Chaucer called it, this fine alloy –
tin, copper, zinc and perhaps silver
hammered out to thin sheets, marked
by dint of the iron hammerhead with mottles
like the moon's face or the armour of a fish.
No lexicographer or chemist knows
how it was made, or how its name was made –
which they spell *latten, laton* or otherwise –
discarded like a fragment of old tin
which I here polish and hold up to the full moon,
its answering talisman, just naming the colour:
not silver, pale gold, mother-of-pearl. Latoun.

On Helm Crag

Height, expressed only in scraps of sound
carried up from the valley: a dog barks,
a motorcycle scores an inch of road
silence resumes; and once a child's shout
cutting thinly across the air
engraves its diamond-scratch on the clear lens
of height, through which all things appear
small and perfect, and myself invisible,
merged an instant into crag and valley
as if I too expected whatever they wait for
to happen the moment I am gone from here.

The Traveller at Yazd

He steps down from the bus
onto dust radiant with spilled oil –
the trance of journey snapped.

Round him, through him, people talk, shout,
an intricate layered trellis of noise.
Luggage is chivvied from the cargo-lockers.

The signs ahead are scarlet Arabic:
a manic exuberant scrawl
like a line of flame on the horizon.

He shoulders his pack. His footsoles
tug into the ground. The street glitters with twilight.
Nobody knows him. This is what he came for.

The Chinese Temple in Hollywood Road, Hong Kong

The dark, the dust. And then the brassy lamps
and red silk banners, muffled voices, flare
of melting candles, and the clack of lots.

Around the shrines, wreckage of joss-stick stubs
as if a colony of birds nested
in the rafters, scattering singed pink twigs,

though only the vast yellow incense-coils
spiral into the shadows overhead,
loading the air with their slow self-consuming.

A bell clangs and an old man hurries past
floundering into a black-and-scarlet robe:
some ritual business waits among the gods,

the sage with domed forehead, the bushy-browed
yellow king or the fishermen's goddess,
Tin Hao, who rides a silver fish like a surfboard.

Somewhere inside this darkness an alchemy
no-one can name or bother to point out
recedes into the gloom, undisturbed.

We never touched it. At the same pace go
the colony, the hoarded pieties,
long life, good fortune, wealth, the ancestors –

rotund, bearded, smiling like Chinese Falstaffs,
they fade into the shadows; perhaps
most truly the gods as we forget about them.

In Europe Everything Has Been Painted

"There are in our countries rivers which have no names, trees which nobody knows, and birds which nobody has described. It is easier for us to be surrealistic because everything we know is new. Everything has been painted in Europe." – *Pablo Neruda*

In Europe everything has been painted.
Let us imagine a region where everything has been painted
and call it Europe. Now what shall we invent
to call America? It might be a woman I am about to discover,
or the revolution, or a land
where there are rivers that have no names
and trees nobody knows, which we must therefore imagine.

And there is Africa, which is marble pavements
cooling under the stars,
sleeping gods with golddust weights
in their ears, white buildings with men on the roofs,
slaveships tearing the sea and lurching at anchor
hurling upwards with the red and blue paint
against the sky, men sick with money and the pox.

Let us invent the mind and call it a fully-evolved
mimic assuming the fractal curve of the snowflake,
blistered paintwork of the toad's skin or the thin
cry of an undescribed bird; irresolute as a dead leaf
or bitter as the migraine-coloured wasp squads
on their house-to-house search of the hollowed pears
strewn in long grass at the edge of summer.

But in Europe the season is over:
they are taking the pictures down from the walls,
the house prepares to fold back into the landscape.
Small birds congregate, to perch among bushes
so exact that even the smallest, sharpest eye
cannot detect the imaginary brushstrokes.

Summer Pudding

for Carole Reeves

Begin with half a pound of raspberries
picked from the deep end of your sloping garden, where the birds
    play hopscotch in the draggled fruitnets; add
a quarter of redcurrants; gently seethe in orange juice
    for six or seven minutes with some sugar,
giving the pan a ritual shake from time to time, inducing
    a marriage of those fine, compatible
tastes; and leave to cool. An open kitchen door invites
    whatever breeze will help itself to flavour,
attenuating it downhill across your neighbours' gardens
    (be generous!) so summer will surprise them,
an unidentifiable recalled fulfilment haunting
    the giant bellflower and the scarlet runners.
Now introduce your strawberries, sliced to let the pallid
    heartsflesh
    transfuse its juice into the mass, transmute
cooled fruit to liquid crystal while you line your bowl with bread
    and add the mixture – keeping back some juice –
lid it with bread, cover and weight it, chill it if you like
    (as if the winter took a hand) and hoard it,
opus magnum ripening its secret, edible,
    inviolable time. And when you dare
slide your knife round its socket to uncling – a sudden suck –
    this gelid Silbury mined with the wealth
of archetypal summer, let it be on one of three
    occasions: for a kitchenful of children
whose mouths grow purpleringed and flecked with whipped
    cream as they dig
    and lose, entranced, the treasure of the minute;
or for the friends around your polished table, when that soft
    lake of mahogany reflects the faces
melting in candlelight and burgundy, rivers of talk
    eddying to a stillness lost in taste
primitive as a language, clear as thought; or for whoever
    will join you in your garden when the sun
carries out summer to the edge of dark, and stay to eat
    there in the early chill as twilight gels
and owlhoots quiver from the gulf of darkness, where a floodlit

    cathedral floats under your eyes, and still
(wreckage of smeared plates and clotted spoons piling the table)
    after the lights are killed and the cathedral
vanishes like a switchedoff hologram, remain to plot
    the moon's progress across the brimming air
scaled by the nightscented stocks, or with binoculars
    arrest the Brownian movement of the stars.

Migraine

    It begins with a cursor,
twinkling flaw in the magic glass of
    vision, a ghost-mote twirling
just off-limits: where you look it still
isn't, but now there's a tease, that haunts
    the confident panning of
your gaze, a dropped stitch threatening the whole
edgeless fabric with dissolution
and it spreads, a no-coloured shining
    seepage, irrational as
a spill of non-Euclidean space
fusing the middle of whatever
you look at: in the road you cross it's
a hole, lively as mirage over
    hot tar (negotiate this
with circumspection, out of it a
car may leap); in the book you read it's
a vibrating black-and-white flamepatch
eating the print – as if into a
pool of tears the next word you want keeps
    weeping itself until you
give up, lie back under a strobing
tornado of zigzags that simmers
down at last to a single chord of
pain, the head ringing drily to a
violin-bow of ache that floats there
like a chainsaw floating through a log.
    No-one can tell what it means
or why it has chosen you. You might
suspect the boiling god of a blocked
inspiration, or guilt over some
archetypal lie; but cheese late at
night, or too much Tia Maria,
seem just as likely. The contingent
demons of physiology spare
    no-one at last; they have no
art; and if this glimpse of the world in
    their distorting lens shows how
brittle our bright arrangements are, with
    that painful wisdom they have,
certainly, done for us all they can.

Snow

Pure as hallucination
the street your steps invade:
houses, building-site, trees,
each twig and girder furred
with its piled thread of snow,
roof and windscreen covered
inch-deep. The same precision
that chased a pane with frost-flowers
sculptures whole landscapes now,
allows no imperfection.

By noon, churned to brown mush
or crusting the frozen gutter
like mucus, it hinders your feet,
though a side-road may still offer
the joy of an untrodden patch
(and the unaccountable urge
to print it with your boot)
and afternoon mist still conjures
lampposts to charcoal smudges
fading out on the day's white page.

Next day, the scrape of shovel
and self-important hum
of the yellow truck spinning out gravel.
Snow starts to forget,
relaxing its frieze of crystal.
Rivers, muddy and turgid,
are hurling themselves seaward:
the pavement-edge gleams wet
where you cross; already under your street
the water gathers momentum.

Russet Apples

Lie back against the pillows:
and again, as if for the first time,
I give you a russet apple.

In our country the custom
is love first, and then apples:
a ritual celebration
of our unhoped-for return
after aeons of wandering where
there was nobody, or the next best thing –

some lover who didn't care
enough to let it be right;
some man who wouldn't trust,
some woman who didn't dare;
where always she was hiding a hate,
or he had to fondle an image
to help him get it on.

Now we've passed the gate,
the land is ours again
and the apple's into the secret;
feel how it loves us as you bite
and the juice comes, cider-sweet,
leaf-sour, and the rusty bronze skin
gleams wet in candle-light,

and feel when I kiss you how
within the mouth's dark space
there is no I or you
but only a fragrance of endless
orchards that waited here, always
ripening, longing to welcome us
back into paradise.

Fidelities

I

A house with a friendly ghost:
he planted columbines in the garden
when he was tenant. After he died
a neighbour saw him look out of the window.
And a child's skeleton
three hundred years old
folded in one of the walls. Maybe the dead
can bear witness. We don't know.
Only it seems something is offered here
out of the long past. We accept it.

II

Tides of meadow lap the garden:
sheep jump the wall
to rip off rosebuds, tender growth-tips
of spinach, lettuce, broadbean.
Moor End Fell is a swell of woodland
to the sky, quilted
with cottongrass, oak, hazel.
The woman who welcomes us here
brings us, with the grace
and also the formality
of a priestess, food: meat; a bowl
of strawberries; homemade Martini.
"Marriage" is a word I savour,
tasting it slowly. So is "husband".
That sounds like a farmer. The first
like a kind of fruit.
A strawberry? Something in season.
"Wife" is firmer, like bread.

III

You drowse behind me on the bed.
Still looped in your heartglow
I sprawl in the window-seat
and read the Arabian Nights,

watching
down the smooth green
trough of the dale
last sun behind Kilnsey Crag:
where a bony elbow of rock
juts through the worn jersey
of bracken, grass, topsoil –
honest for once.
From the sky's deepening blue-green solution
stars crystallise out.

IV

We come over the top
and the next valley tilts towards us
a veined cup of stone and grass,
the far side glassy with distance,
the village caught like grit
at the bottom.
          These friable stone houses;
and a blind white horse on the green
noses its way darkling
among thistles, ryegrass, bubbles of dandelion –
lipping the great circle of its tether.

V

Ravaged with ivy,
a secretive inn
where the kegs stand on the floor behind the bar;
the landlord circles tables with an enamel jug,
his ear atilt
to the TV set on the counter
where England are winning the Test at Headingley
on Botham's innings. Indifferent
to cricket, we breathe the excitement,
sharing a ritual
with the few customers. They let us be included, who
enjoy their elation, then our own.
As the match ends
there is laughter, scraping of chairs,

assessment of play. Nothing
shakes an essential silence
founded deeper than the stone flags under our feet.
From the wall opposite
sepia faces gaze out:
a rabbit-shoot. Lined up
for the photographer, they stand
at attention: expressionless, moustached,
twenty men
holding up countless rabbits
in rows, strung together
by the ears, like long furry
garlands looped
from hand to hand;
their own monument, not
asking for our approval.

VI

A buffetting wind:
at closing time
we find the road carries us
at once away from all that, fronting
the hillside, to cross a yard
(the ragged
timeless barking of farmdogs)
and take the bridleway
along the slope's edge
until the village drops back into the pocket
of the fell,
and we climb up into a path that leads
through the eye of a stile chipped from the stone skyline
and on like a thread
into the rest of our days.

Signal

Like a faint sonar in the night
I read your signal now, a light
Quick quiver come and gone within
The echoing depth under the skin
When my love guides my fingers to
The depth where she has sounded you.
Heavy between the tides of sleep
We wait, and feel again the deep
Disturbance gathering to break
The surface of our lives and shake
A world of habits to the strange
Designs of unpredicted change.
   Now in your secret chemical garden
Bones crystallise and muscles harden,
Directions of the will begin
To try the walls that wrap you in
And turn about below the heart
To which you beat a counterpart.
Small Jonah in the lovely whale,
You will forget to tell your tale:
What led you to these human shores,
What other name and form were yours,
What storms of fear and longing drove
Towards the little bait of love
We scattered in pure ignorance,
Caught in our senseless lovers' trance.
   And now we turn again to sleep,
Under the film of dreams I keep
A sense of your live touch, that lifts
Towards us, empty-handed, gifts
Of pain and transformation, our new
Selves as strange to us as you.

Little Girl on the Lawn

She is afraid of the grass
and sits alone without moving, her
right foot held delicately,
awkwardly, up out of reach
of those rippling green tongues.

Perhaps there is too much space:
the sky is enormous blue,
the snakeskin towers of lupin
rocket into the air
their strident pinks and purples

and under the glare of sun
her mother and I are calling
out on the shimmering green
ocean where she fears
to be lost; and so she cries

and keeps her small right foot
aloft still as an amulet,
uncommitted, her own, and will not
let it step into the world
in which we have long since drowned.

Leaf Wading

For the first time she can walk
Under October trees
And feel the leaves with a soft strange shock
Crowd like a wave to her knees.

Reaching the end of the drift
She stands and considers, then
Turns back with an urge of sudden delight
To trudge through it again,

And this rare afternoon
In the brittle gold sun
Invents for herself what all children
Always have done.

"Look"

i

Only the eye can talk
about the glitter of silk:
kept in the memory, under glass,
like flowers or feathers it fades
to a merely average brightness
until you turn again to look
and the seeing like a spark
ignites the same flame-radiance.

ii

I can compare it only
to a February fall of snow
that wakes us early with importunate light
so that the eye shrinks and thought is postponed,
but we stand at the window holding the curtain
longer than usual, while for a moment
vision drinks the sheer brightness
as if slaking a thirst we didn't know was there,
after which we turn back to the room
with our like or our dislike of snow.

Monuments

> "As soon as we have the thing before
> our eyes, and in our hearts an ear
> for the word, thinking prospers."
> – Martin Heidegger

I

Perfect curve, shaped like nothing
but itself. Love-object, disquieting muse:
little paraboloid moon
pored like skin, freckled lightly
at the south pole, sheened
ceramic. Cold to touch as stone. Something
rolled in sleep; weighty
in the hand. Pink tear-plummet from eye
of soft rock god. Friendly face
all gaze, no feature. Inside, messy life.

II

The sky blue tortoiseshell.
Mixed on its palette the curded marquetries
and stones, the scumbled
rag and piled muscle, a slow
pondering manoeuvre
on the estuary. Fingernail flecks,
apricot-vanilla scoop
stealing a march; the fibreglass
escarpment pitched
on a silent thunder of frozen surf.

III

Flame of deepening shadow, flexible
razor. Flat smokeplume
flaring from tapered, curvate spine; airstream
grafted to slick, horny rod. Lightshot,
silkwatered, these elastic
shreds so easily peeled
apart, as easily drawn
into an unflawed blade. A little

fluff at the base, then the clean blunt
shaft, translucent, durable and light as a proverb.

IV

Creased like a soft leather
with folding – those grained, wispy trackways
crossing a rose plain etched like a banknote
to Maori swirl of lines.
Blue cords knit and webbed under
taut, plied surface. Five branches
curl, cantilevered from central pad;
on one, askew, a gold quoit, alien metal
in this soft island. Open, meaning something –
direction, offer, welcome. A riddle, closed.

V

Sheer urgency in one direction, still
and to the point. Swordfry. Midflight arrow
secreting a drop of space
like a tear in its eye, its tiny noose, emptyface
under a bright hood, thirled
by the compacted thread. Spine
of steeltree, polished slipway
for light, cherishing fineness
towards a touchable
end that tempts, hurts like an unlit flame.

VI

Answer. Solution. Secret. Brass
gollywog. Soft notched saw.
Tarnished bar bitten
across its grooves to a mountain-range
profile of broken teeth, indentures
binding to a remote
partner of cryptic inner ways coded
along that metal graph
like a brief song in notation, a flourish
followed by tumblers, the obedient tongue.

VII

Magic painting-book:
on a wet-ink sky
light's watercolours come clear, a hoop
of soft neons, green
the most prominent. There are no ends –
where the buildings start it simply
isn't, nothing moves and now it
wastes into air, the grey-pearl cloudbanks
or the mind's eye, an afterimage
that fades in the fixing.

VIII

Out of that tarblack pigtail pours a peacock-
blue curve up into soft
flirting spire. Lightdipped brushtip
juggling a dimmer, hazed loop in its tongue, lapping
stirred air over its shed, glassy
pool. Crisis on a tower.
The crater's lip holding, holding until
(Rapunzel!) a clear plait sinews
down, bulges, sets
to a fine rib on the ivory wall.

IX

Furled labyrinth of stained
pages, veined and deckled watercolour
or fine ink, alluring spiral to crumpled
infinities of implication, book
reconstituted from dimensions
beyond us: you compel
apostrophe and reverence. I drink you
deep in a whole breath and you're untouched:
ragged and flawless,
you promise and contain everything and have no inside.

X

Through a film of dust the finger
draws a clear furrow of bright nothing.
Those metallic specks and blemishes:
sunspots on a slice of vertigo
I pass from hand to hand. Ceiling
at the bottom of a well
flat on the table, light's
skating-rink, perception's
uneasy joke. Bending gingerly
towards me, the not-quite-unfamiliar face.

Lamp and Bright Page

Lamp and bright page,
how many times
I come here for comfort,
for effort – and to delay
as well, for rather than write
I open some book
and read uneasily
with half a mind until the cat climbs
into my light and sits
on the paper, chin lifted
towards me, the great eyes
mooning expectancy
and bafflement at what it is
takes my attention
so far away from her,
so far from myself.
   I too am baffled,
and if I knew the answer
could gather her into my lap
and read on, I would not care
how far past midnight,
instead of pushing her away,
her and the book
to stare again at the depths
of midnight and lamplight –
the mind's eye wide as a cat's –
awaiting the resolution,
the sudden clearing of sight
and words written somewhere
on the lost pages of mind.

II

Vignettes

*Poems for Twenty-One Wood Engravings
by Thomas Bewick*

I

Out of some dream I wake to find myself
here between two blows of the sledge,
my task to break large stones to small stones
to be trodden under the horses' feet, chewed
by carriagewheels. The blackbird's curious eye
marks me when I look up. I throw myself into the stroke,
swing up again and he is still there
unmoved. The road like a river
turns its corner. When the shadows have turned
I shall eat dinner on the bank
staring at road metal,
pick, shovel and sledge.
Then hands will shape again to the helve,
smashed rock alternate
with a glimpse of the unsplintered world:
a windmill fading into the white sky,
a signpost pointing to nowhere and nowhere.

II

Wielding anger like a favourite stick
apt to the hand, this pursy driver
flogs his rawboned horse. Stupidity incarnate,
dully relishing the world's hatefulness.
Patient and poised over his wood block
Bewick has time to notice the trunk's end
scored with thud of axe, rip of saw;
the beechgrain patterned like a fingerprint;
also the wheel blocked by a stone
and a sign on the cart that says WOOD. Beyond them,
the natural destination of such moods:
gateshaped, also made of wood, the gallows.

III

A hard wind charges. We hurl into it,
galloping in a dream to bluster
flat a fieldful of Boney's arrogant French.
They surge around us, shout
and crash in the green spray of spring
the wind flings over the branches. Tom
leads with his cornet, heels
spurring his mount, muddying the scuffed letters.
Death or glory!
                    In the big house, fires
still crackle. Under the library window
the atlas incubates
in its folio index villages no-one has heard of –
Omdurman, Passchendaele, Quatre-Bras.
Repeat their names: we cannot hear you
or wake from our time; only ride on,
distant and fictional as the famous dead.

IV

No-one knows where I am.
Out at the edge of the world
I sit; I could go on walking
until home dwindled to nothing.
Already our house is small
as a penny loaf. If I turn
I see it over my shoulder. I can cover it with my thumbnail
then let it creep out: that notch
is the wicket gate; that thread
the smoke from Nancy's oven. I close one eye
and when the wind tugs
the housewall bulges
like a white bubble. Will father see
I have left the gate open? Does he know
I can go on walking for ever
until the thread from the house will snap
and we shall be free, my stick, my dog and me?
The wind rattles. Shall I turn back,
or go on and be free?

V

If all the world were paper, all the sea
ink, the magpie would be king. Meanwhile,
Pica pica, with his copperas-green
tail, black coat and bands of glossy linen,
swaggers: he's dandy, doctor, lawyer, parson,
mountebank among birds. What does he hunt –
ink, poison or cordial? Cocks his head
as the prize sails nearer. Rippling
from page to printed page, the ink pursues
that wry intentness, pen or graver darting
bird-beak-quick to trap the tempting image –
printing the streambank, hopping at the gleam
of its own craft caught in that shining bottle.

VI

Pushing through a weather of his own,
wrapped in hard luck as in a cloak,
here comes the man no-one can blame
looking for work again. Will he stop at your gate?
He is preoccupied with his own story
and will tell you some of it if you ask,
though you will know him none the better for it.
He will work aptly and without enjoyment,
talk little, looking beyond you,
reserving judgement, being in the right.
When someone falls from the ladder
in the rickyard, or the bank fails
and the mortgage is foreclosed,
it will not be his fault, though just his luck,
he will say, as he leaves. He will come
when you are short-handed. You will listen
to his tale and hesitate. Possibly,
against your better judgement, will take him on,
telling yourself that what you feel is sympathy.
If you get what you deserve, do not blame him.

VII

I am John Cowie of Ovington,
late of Napier's Granadiers,
and these the hat and coat I wore
at Minden, Wilhelmsthal
and Warburg. Where no musket ball,
sabre or shell could find a way
now wind tugs through and rain drips
and ripe mould like velvet grows.
We trod those other fields
to mire, and slept head against stone,
savour of earth in our nostrils – but what
I saw there, no-one shall know:
I have no restless dreams where I lie
under the snug blanket of earth;
and now the coat is more use than the man,
emptily scaring a last enemy,
half its brass buttons stolen by boys
and all the field under its arms.

VIII

I cross your path an instant
as you walk the wood, wrapped in daydream.
Do you not know me? Poised
on this shard of timber I gaze
into you. Not a muscle
or a whisker moves. We wait
here in the moment, our eyes
meeting in strangeness, while a birdcall
echoes in the spacious roof of branches.
The flick of a leaf, a spring
and I am gone, slipping
into the thickets of your memory.
We shall meet again. You walk on:
all around you the wood is alive.

IX

Midsummer rain, melting
all the eye sees to a plash of pewter:
grey metal sky, tarnished puddles,
the stoic windmill and stone post.
We give up pacing our own hoofprints, give up
cautiously lipping the mulch of dung, straw, grass-stalk,
mud. Rain goes on for ever: impossible
to look at anything else. But the nostril
tells other tales: the herby tang of clods
opening their mineral coolness; swirls
and shifts of air flavoured with damp bark
from dripping hedgebanks; spacious cold from the uplands;
a meadowful of green barley, simmering.
Endure, endure. We take what's given, content
though our bodies turn to mud statues and rain
carves and carves its ridges into our coats.

X

I meet myself again.
Once I would run this way
and pass some old man poking the grass
with a stick, his mind idling
on epitaphs. What did I hold? A kite
sometimes, or a top. But mostly
ran with a hoop. My wrist still feels the knack of it.
My eyes fell on this Latin spell
that conjured everything. A dream!
It is all exactly the same,
only we have changed places:
my fingers harden round the stick
and here is summer again, and a boy
bowling a hoop like a zero towards nothing –
his mindless joy, my memories,
the world's full circle.

XI

Shared guilt and excitement rope you
in, your circle pressing and toppling
towards a mystery:
iridescence of cockcrow
shrunk to a bundle of dirty feathers
twitching and tumbling across the ring.
All shoulders and elbows, one
bearing another down, you jostle
and gape, treading blood and spilt beer
into the mud. That dark whirlpool keeps
your eyes from the rainbow; though its ample
hoop stays clear as a promise
against the inklined sky, radiant with all
the seven colours of imagination.

XII

Waste sea, waste shore, paid for
in the chipped coin of shellfish prised,
chucked into the creel, rattling
like pebbles in tidesuck when you shake them down.
Seawind flavoured with absence,
cloud, gullcry over rock
scours you, the accustomed
watching for son and husband,
the price of the catch; a firm abrasion
of all that doesn't matter. The tide
is spilling into the land, the hard sandribs
melting and rippling. You raise a song,
every note of it earned and priceless.

XIII

Heaped with black fossil
wherries in cortege
ride the Tyne stylish as swans,
and coals leave Newcastle
to sow petrific forests
over England. The treeferns
of smoke, the thickets of chimneys
are climbing the air. Already
men have spun an iron web
across the gorge at Coalbrookdale.
A boundary stone like a graveslab
commemorates outmoded
heraldry; soon windmill and sailbarge
will look quaint as castles,
dwindling and glimmering across the fields' green table.
Into the toybox with them!
Out of the carboniferous rock
the steam engine clambers. The new age has begun.

XIV

Somewhere, ridiculously, a wrong turning;
how long have you been watching this?
Surely overhead it is still afternoon,
long sun slanting over the flowerpots,
the poplars shimmering behind the glassed frames.
Admit a repetitious fascination
in the pedantic accuracy
of the monkey interminably basting that joint;
still, it is time you were gone. Now concentrate.
Imagine yourself getting out of the chair; imagine
yourself turning round; now for the hundredth time try
to imagine your way out through the shadows behind you.

XV

Autumn is where things start.
About the equinox
a balance shifts: the unsettled land
tousled by rain and gales,
the trees shouldering off summer and the birds agitated,
everything moving. A time
for cardgames, portents,
turning over the accounts, taking
augury as the birds migrate.
Do not mistake the season's tang
for death's: even now
like some demotic emblem
dropped from the zodiac,
husband and midwife on the one horse
gallop ungainly
towards a birth, though perspectives
change at once and a whirling leaf
swallows them. Now choose
your talisman for the dark months:
that which survives the snow will rule next year.

XVI

Dish and chamber-pot:
between them the body's life
allowed for, grudgingly.
But the mind is judged
healthier in abstinence,
its diet a shaft of sunlight,
stone roof, stone walls, this chain –
though pacing out in thought
who knows what shrinking labyrinth
of grievance or fantasy?
Only history seems on his side:
somewhere impatient Reason is bursting prison gates,
her maenad throng rampaging
along the corridors.
Reason, that guileless goddess:
with ineluctable logic she advances,
every moment
halving and again halving
her distance from this door.

XVII

How easily the rich man enters the eye
of the peacock: bright, hard, reflective,
measuring a prudent distance;
bothered about his dignity, and my dog.
I blot the landscape cheerfully; wonder
who wraps himself in these unruffled lawns,
park and woodland fanned out round him, textured
with bird and poplar, the world his prospect,
secluded by the haha of money
from vulgar crowding. If I fought his battles
it was just so that such as he
need never notice such as I. Should I blame him, or myself?
If I had his wealth, would I do as he does?
I am human, therefore divided.

XVIII

Emptied by snow, the fields
grow stranger at twilight, detail
of ploughland, bracken and ditch blanked out
to a clean space you can only disturb.
The clumped sheep have their dole of hay:
now you walk back,
the loudest sounds your dog's breath
as he paddles nimbly on the drifts
and the creak of your boots,
every lift of the foot flinging a divot of snow.
From the village, hugging its light and warmth,
not a gleam nor a voice.
Even the mill quiet as a stopped clock.
You quicken your pace. Beside you
your earlier bootprints
look different already, pressing
away into the dark
like the tracks of someone else, who has not returned.

XIX

Why do we delight
in his poise – this boy
who must not falter, balanced, a
small quotidian god
between the stones and the corded box,
between Atlas and Narcissus,
who cannot rest his load
anywhere, or look too long
for his own face, surprised
between footfalls? Is it our want
of the simplicity
the moment leaves to him,
where there is only the task, single
mind and surefoot body
and on the stones no-one to speak of
until the box thuds on the bank
and the arms are allowed to ache?
Or is it that watching him we see
plainly and with a kind of
joy, that for us too there is no turning back?

XX

My kayak beached on snow
a fallen moon behind me, I strike out
sure as a compass-needle for the pole.
If they should call me back
still these rare magnetic wastes
are proof against all voices.
Purchas, Hakluyt,
your books are laid aside at last.
No-one recounts this journey.
Past, the tropics of fever
shaking their sick brocade;
past, too, the morass of the body.
Ahead, only glass cliffs
and snow like a pillow. Here
I leave no footprints. Never to have existed
is all I ask, the mind's mirror to stay
unclouded by the faintest breath
of memory. Friend,
you who come towards me,
take my weapons. The boat
is ready. Let it carry you to life.
When you wake you will have forgotten me.

XXI

At the far end of time's telescope,
Thomas Bewick, you come into sight
Resolved by the sharp focus of those two
Best lenses, history and imagination,
To move like one of your own vignettes
After the book is closed. Here is Cherryburn,
And you sent supperless to bed for some
Boyhood insolence or recklessness,
Lying awake and "listing with delight" –
From the little window at your bedhead –
"The murmuring or roaring of the burn
In flood"; or watching at that same window
Morning after morning when you woke
"All the varying seasons of the year"
Transform themselves in a kaleidoscope
Of mist and rain, leafcolour and human
Occupation, the pane etched by frost somedays
Or beaded out of true by the refractory
Raindrops.   Here, as apprentice,
You walk the riverbank from Newcastle
Watching the town boys sliding on ice

"Smooth, almost, as a Seeing Glass"
Or in summer stop by the sides of woods
"To admire the dangling woodbine and roses
Spangled or powdered with pearly drops of dew";
And last, at your workshop in St Nicholas' Churchyard,
Under the adequate, mysterious Northern light
You peer, rapt, into the black slice
Of polished boxwood like a pool of ink
Where such a scene floats clear and steadies, while
With a repeated urging of the hand –
Palm snug against the graver's handle –
You coax it from the darkness, crystalline
With long immersion in your memory.
   You were cantankerous over money,
Held theories about Monarchy and God,
Were quick to sense an insult; and as surely
As Blake or Palmer, traced one of the heavens,
That place where by sheer clarity of detail
All things become their archetypes. You would
Grumble at how I trespass through your fields
Though leaving not a footprint nor a blade
Of all your wiry grass disturbed. A ghost,
I take my leave. This lens falls out of line,
We're back with words. The cat climbs to my knee.
Outside the window, white October sky.
Sparrows vibrate and squabble in the eaves.

III

The Barrel-Dance

For a year I lived over a pub.
Monday and Wednesday mornings
I worked with half a mind, my ear
attuned to the traffic's rumblings
in the street, awaiting the warm beat
of an engine idling below:
the brewery wagon. When it came,
the world opened and I was at the window
to watch the new barrels unloaded –
not your spry aluminium kegs
but all the dead weight of iron hoop and wood
stave, and about nine gallons of beer:
a weight that if one of them took
a sudden drop could crush a man's foot
and crack the paving-stone under it.

The driver would climb up over
the tailboard, sing out for the landlord
and then with a roll and a toss
spring the first barrel over the side
of the wagon and down to his mate
who'd catch it as it fell
with a thud that shook the building
on a coconut-fibre pad at his feet
and spinning the cask on one rim
skate it towards the cellar
like a weightless dancing-partner
and juggle it horizontal to roll down the chute.

I thought no dancer or acrobat
could match the rhythm of their work,
their art of weight and movement,
but like all performing artists
they improved the world not a jot:
I never drank in the pub,
for the landlord remained a churl
and the beer in his glasses warm and flat.

Caption

Photograph of a corner-shop, its rust-red
paintwork framing a collage of gaudy
adverts, *Brooke Bond Tea, Senior
Service Satisfy, Tizer, Park Drive*
on the windows, and the interior beyond
cool blue-green like an aquarium.
A hoop-backed upright chair on the paving-stones
recalls the old woman who sat like a doll
there one hot day, eyes closed to the light,
thin wrists composed on knees, completing
my picture, I thought, until I returned
with a camera and she was gone,
just the chair keeping its spindly shadow
at the edge of the stone doorstep.
   Park Street or Albert Street, one of the places
you couldn't find now under the rubble
of demolition and the cleared earth even
with a map, any more than now
I could trace to some junk-shop that cheap
wooden chair which waits in the photograph,
stage-left, the seat still cool in the sun, for someone
who in a moment will step again
into the street and rest there.

Buying Valentines

Months can surprise us: today,
for instance, cold February holds
so many aces in her hand:
the shops blush and billow with hearts,

vermilion, cherry and lavender hearts,
all colours of the candy-spectrum –
even a few in lace. A chorus
of little whores, singing of how

you can earn love, or buy, it will be like this:
a calendarful of lipstick kisses,
sweet hearts that open for your inspection,
a mere date making a new mistress.

And February always brings them:
these paper hearts will perish, perish
and yet come back yearly like leaves
unfolding in their short season

and we buy them, thinking it's a year
since last we bought such innocence,
glad no-one will open them unwillingly
unlike letters or telegrams,
or other cards the months deal out.

Dictionary

Weighing perhaps ten pounds, it makes the desk
an altar. Other books and casual objects
   congregate themselves around it.

It is a god: I can place anything,
whether a grand piano or a microscope
   beside it, sure without checking

that inside those black covers it is named.
I can perform no action which this oracle
   cannot define and number

and ratify by quoted precedent.
I imagine the books on my shelves feeling humbled:
   it swallowed them all before they existed,

its belly contains infinite others like them.
Only by gibberish could they excape,
   and scarcely then: it defines *Jabberwock*,

and *gobbledeygook* (substantive, US slang)
and knows who coined the words, which it takes as tribute.
   It is alpha and omega.

Where shall we go to escape the eye of the god
which is Word? Into our dreams, perhaps,
   the love and confusion we can't express,

for if we say them the book will swallow them
as (and here I feel a certain frustration)
   it has already swallowed this poem,

motionless and emotionless as God.
I struggle to breathe parts of it into life.
   The dumb, idiot book says nothing.

Ovid in Exile

At the outposts of a broken language
I have lived lately. These barbaric provinces:
the worst wine in the empire, no books, and the most
execrable climate. (I have a few notes of
such grammar as persists here, having to instruct
my servants. His Imperial Highness would not
be interested.) A poem will not suffice
for this bone-grasping cold, let alone
death or loneliness. Like the provincials,
such things would need physical violence
to make them intelligible. The grunts
of these oxen express them more accurately.

As for you, Julia, if you expect a poem
you can go to the Emperor and let him
fondle you with his greasy hexameters.

Winter Poem for Osip Mandelstam

I light a lamp by the white wall,
my breath steams in the empty rooms.
There was no warmth in your exile

but as I move in this cold house
to think of you seems natural
as making light in a dark place.

I remember how you refused to stop –
resting your paper on the lid of a suitcase,
writing poems while the stars sat up

(as you put it) like little bureaucrats
who watched you getting your world into shape
as they yawned over their nightly reports.

They buried you in their drifts of paper
but under that snow of blanks your words
repeat themselves, a White Paternoster

to charm the blood back to its course
from all the internal wounds of Russia.
The rivers move under their ice:

the only strategy is persistence
in winter, to expect no sudden rescues.
Change is the task of the hardest seasons.

Ampersand

"And *per se* and", the grammarians,
the stammering pedants, christened you at first,
but at your usual short-cut game
you slipped a syllable, old escapist,
to come out like a clown with a clown's name.

I remember you in black on primrose,
twenty-seventh in my Edwardian alphabet book,
drawn as a snake tied in a knot with a grin
on its face, which pleased me more than the innocent
B-for-Baker or S-for-Sailorman.

I find you like a trickster in other guises:
rampant in gold on book-jackets as
a back-to-front 3 with a foot in the air;
or scrawled like a plus-sign by people who
don't know what you're called and don't care;

but that's all right. You'll cross any frontier
in Europe. Convenience will see you through.
Typeface jester, strange hunchback,
camp-follower of the alphabet,
our laziness & haste curl up in you.

Mirror and Candle

The mirror and the candle throw
their incantation through the room
and on the wall our shadows loom
monstrous in their reverberate glow.

Their occult transformations make
our bed a range of hills, the floor
a flickering plain edged with the shore
that borders on a glassy lake.

We act our legends in that space.
The mirror takes, the candle gives,
and light from both the eye receives
to conjure out that doubled place

where through the sky our shadows pass
drowned in the depths that wait below.
I rest my cheek on the pillow
and in the fathoms of the glass

you reach across the dark to me.
The light flows back the way it came.
High on its tower of wax the flame
sings songs of mutability.

The Hands

Busy and blindfold, taught their trade by trial
and touch, they are naturals, eager exponents
of every half-formed thought, or of no thought.
Getting bored, they twiddle their thumbs or tap,
thinking that you are thinking nothing,
waiting to run an errand to pen or pocket.

The devil, we say, finds work for idle hands.
Idle heads will dream their own contraptions
but wreak no havoc till hands are called to service:
hands in hatred of hands hammered iron
nails into the palms, twisted a crown,
offered the dice their chance to make decision.

The pride of heads denies them understanding
then reaches out a hand to prove the world,
explain its music and articulate
precise intelligence of love. The dark,
the silent, all comply to the hand's order,
make their confession to the fingertips

as honest as those bluntly-put enquiries.
No artists, they'll create by mere assuming
as they assume you now, love, substance you
out of the night's negations. Magic of touch,
you're there again. I feel you reach towards me.
The darkness round us sings the praise of hands.

The Tattooist

She asked me for a butterfly
there, on her shoulder. No-one knows
what goes on under the skin.
I was a man with time to kill
for money, and an art to sell,
patient enough with my line
to take the minimum of pain
filling a chosen space
and never choosing the design.

I worked at a square inch,
a needle nuzzling the skin.
I wiped the blood off where the line
was drawn, a blue embroidery
in the margin of her world.
She paid, and I am free to stay
like the icecream man and the clairvoyante
and the others who sell their addictions,
and she goes wrapped in the new web of her body:
she will never be naked again.

Bluebeard's Wife

Like Alice, I stepped into a cool mirror
to a place where the clock had a smiling face,
to a garden of talking flowers:
but when I walked the paths to meet you
began the game of hide and seek and
further you withdrew at every step
(O master of the primal mansion), further,
to tower over the trembling land
like a mirage of God on the sky, and all the while
a bunch of keys sang "Bluebeard" in your hand,

"Bluebeard", they whispered, and the more I loved,
more I was drawn into the dark of eyes'
fathomless pupils, drowning,
swimming down until something was solid inside.
Like a small fish I curled at night
warm on a pulsing pillow,
dreaming in the red chambers of a heart,
the soft walls soothing as they surged apart

and closed again. I was a child exploring:
rooms opened into rooms, and in my hand
the keys sang at each door and charmed the lock;
rooms of the throat, the skin, the womb
unfolded, offered themselves to me,
and still I was alone until the last
door opened and I found you small and face
to face, staring at me as at a glass.
I touched you, but you didn't notice.
Now I shall leave the house and set you free.

The Tell-Tale Heart

No need to tell how long he had endured
the old man's raving. It seemed at last he must have
grown thoroughly inured.

He would sit up, when ordered, half the night;
would check the tyrant's figures, copy his cramped notes
by meagre candlelight.

Charged with deceit or sloth, he gave no sign
of anger, fingers steady on the account-book
ruling the black line

with never a smudge of sweat. At most, by chance
catching the maid's eye, he would enlist her
sympathy with a glance.

A single murmur would have meant the sack.
Who knows what sudden snarl, what final flung word
broke this poor drudge's back?

He spent this morning by the lake. Somehow
small pressures build. He walks at last with firm tread
back to the house. And now,

some slowly-growing want at last obeyed,
carefully he unlocks the desk drawer,
pensively thumbs the blade.

The Core

Cut through an apple, and you find a star.
There is a mathematics of design
and symbol in the artifice of nature:
the fall that shook the fruit from Newton's tree
pulls down the meteor, and for a sign
the apple keeps its hidden signature,
an asterisk embedded in the heart
referring to a single symmetry
beyond the laws that cut the world apart.

Shropshire Union Canal

This unexpected night,
warmer by five degrees,
cleared the coal-heaps of white,
thawed out the iced-up quays

and unobtrusively
without a jolt or shock
set the canal-boats free
and opened every lock.

IV

Tourists

Tourists

A chisel nudging stone, chasing a curve
Out to the corner of the block, an eye
Slant to the line that draws it and the grain
Running its whorls to ripple in the face,
The mallet tapping measure, measure, measure,
Chipping an echo from a distant wall.

I walk along a flat beach where flat shells
Blink up to light under a spill of wave
And cloud back into sand. My footprints fill
And melt, fill and melt. Into the surf
I wade and dangle shoulder-deep in blood-
Warm water. Fish embellish the glass depth
Under me, dodging fissures of sunlight,
Winking and darting, and I think and think,
Treading the water, wondering how far
Jakarta is, whether there is a doctor,
Or will the fever burn itself away –
So easy to imagine things are better
Today, a little better, treading water
Because there's nothing else to tread. Then walk
Up the steep current sucking round my feet
Against the sand to lie in the hot beach
And let this tedious mind be blank as water.

At Ubud after rain a cock stepped out
Onto the path between the dripping leaves
And took his survey of the garden while
Red flowers and spiders' webs beaded and trilled
With water, picked his way along the stone
Slabs of the alley, and we drank our tea
Lulled by a stillicide of drinking garden,
Forest unfurling in the scope of rain,
The quarreyfall of soft receding thunder.
   Rusty jangle of the cock's throat
Broke up the air, a garish chord floated
And dropped abruptly as begun, flaring
From the next compound and the other cocks
Further across the village in a jagged
Ripple of sound that vanished at the edge

Of hearing, or the place where houses stopped
Before the forest.
                    By the road, old men
Sit in the shade and talk and knead their fingers
Loving and restless in the birds' long feathers,
Preening and coaxing. If you stop, will spread
A wing like an array of knives or ruffle
The golden cowl that shivers round the neck,
Turning the beak up while a stiff red tongue
Quivers, and the unashamed black eye
Floats in its ring of red and takes you in.

By the dirt road, outside the temple gate.

Every temple festival starts with a cockfight.

Every temple has its empty platforms
That wait until the festival for gods
To occupy them, under thatched awnings.
And the gods wait inside the carved stones,
The traffic islands with their four faces,
The glaring guardians on the bridge-piers,
Or in the air the smaller spirits playing
About the village, who appreciate
Palmleaf offerings set out at the threshold
Plaited or folded with a flower, a sweet;
Or on the dashboard of the taxi.

                            Clear
Patience the stone, fretting into event.

I have no patience. This will make three days
That you've been ill. I bring you tea and check
(As best I can) your temperature, wrist
Against your wet forehead. Still too hot,
You have no appetite, your head still aches
At times. You want to stay there in the dark.
You don't feel *too* bad. Is it any better?
Maybe, maybe. To kill the time I eat
My way down a long menu, every meat
In peanut oil and coconut oil and garlic,
And watch the sun drop in the milky sea.

Nothing to do but lie and feel your arms
Tender and damp beside me in the dark,
This way and that way on the cotton blanket.
There is neither electricity nor clean water.

Blind cells in rock were cut for forest hermits
Up in the mountains, centuries ago,
A few steps from the door we were in darkness
Until the eye relaxing coalesced
Outline of a stone bed, stone doorway
Leading again into another darkness.
Spreading fingers at the wall, we found
Not fear, some solid and familiar truth
As in a workroom. This way and that, the mind
Tugs the world over us like a blanket
And you forget touching whatever it
Meant, the laps of sleep are solacing
Our hunger for a foothold in the path
Of sliding sand and up the live volcano
We walked, leaving the small town assembled
Around the flank, caught frailly in a soil
Whose only growth was oranges and cabbages,
Where oranges and cabbages were all
For sale in the bleak market on the edge
Of chasms of white mist, and in the chill
Every damp morning people wandered by
Hunched up in coloured towels or grey blankets
Coughing in mist until the sun at noon
Cleared the crater and burnt it all away.
And if we walked there in the afternoon
Up the one street between the shacks of concrete
And painted tin the bristling dogs flew out
Snarling and clattering behind our feet
Just out of kicking distance. In the Losmen
Batur Sari we bargained over grainy
Coffee and banana-mango pancakes
With Gedé (autodidact, almost
The town headman, adventurer who'd learned
The tourist languages and worked as guide,
I now think, to explore people like us)
To guide us up the peak, to start at dawn;
Slept in damp blankets with a smell of mushrooms.

Agung was miles of dusty earth and scrub
Turning to crusted ash drifted with flower
Of sulphur, yellow ripples in the grey
Speckled with tiny pumicestones like charred
Sponges. The sole sank in at every step,
The sandals filled, and yet the foot enjoyed
A warm, dry, soft, inhuman purity;
And where we rested Gedé played his flute,
Teasing out echoes from the lower rocks,
A fluttering counterpoint launched in abrupt
Smooth fragments over fields of curdled mist
A thousand feet below.
                      Your coolie hat
Bobbed like a lantern up the blinding track
Floating its disc of shade, a dazzle-patch
Before my feet, until the path expired
And there were the craters, tidy conic sections
Duned and gently vapouring, lemongrey
Soft edges honed to the impeccable
Poise of an hourglass drift, where nothing happened;
Then we turned back and hardedged spokes of light
Began to rule and slice the heads of mist
And a dark gathering in the white confusion
Focused itself down to a turquoise lake

From which a man under a wooden yoke
Was carrying water in two dripping tins
To feed his rows of cabbages, ranked
In the fine soil down to the water's edge.

From a small dugout, plainly a thick grey
Irony treetrunk chopped into a blunt
Kind of boatshape, a man in a knitted rainbow
Cap, Peruvian somehow, cast and paid
Invisibly a line into the water.

A single ripple, larger, larger, nothing.

I watch the darkness like a wall of rock
Pitted with stars or phosphenes, maze
Of leaves and fragments until memory
Steadies a moment in another forest

Where I strayed on ahead of you and found
A clearing open under the cliff face
And on a shelf cut shallow in the rock
A small stone figure with the hands upturned,
The meditation-posture, a smile
Traced or imagined in the rock, the nose
Broken away the only sign of roughness,
The rounded limbs smooth as a stone child's.
    A pause like waiting centuries, silence
Met in the face of stone, and in the silence
A forest sparkling with the noise of birds.
I put a white flower on the upturned hands
(It looked as if the wind had blown it there).

Daylight, and while you half-rest I go out –
Drawing a draggle-tail of village children –
To find help or advice, which should be near,
Think of it: this group of huts exists
For visitors to stay in. They serve food,
There's a concrete platform with a shower,
One or two villagers speak English or German.
I talk to them, and when I ask advice,
Kindly, perplexed, they draw away, faces
Gentle and impenetrable. We're
Turist, a word the same in every language,
Therefore unreal, out beyond a gap
No-one can cross, figures inside a mirror.
At last I find a boy willing to listen
And try his English far enough to tell me
There's a pharmacy in Singaraja.

I find it: a neat shop close to the market,
Behind the counter two girls in white coats.
Smiling, they diagnose "Bali fever";
Reach a white package down from a high shelf.

I hitch a lift on someone's motorbike
Along the forest road, under the palms.
The usual questions: how old am I? Then,
How many children? I shout back my answers,
No, I'm not married, yes, my wife is ill –
The engine thuds and labours as we dodge

Potholes and boulders in the road. A soft
Handshake, and I take the hairline path
Between two ricefields to our group of huts.
An easy triumph. So you take a pill
And try a walk under the arched palms.
Pallor and sweat, you're beautiful. We talk
About a swim tomorrow, and some food,
Something to drink besides warm tea. Quite soon
The fever drops, then keeps on coming back.
We keep on hoping, and maintain the dose
Because there's nothing else to do.
                                    Hours later
After the early dark has dropped its bag
Over us, I interrogate the label –
Guttering oil-lamp, indistinct small print,
Unrecognisable language, out of which
A single word comes clear: *salicylate*.
Aspirin. It isn't going to work.

It rains again (this is the rainy season),
A dull groundbass on sand, concrete, bamboo
And corrugated metal, where the mind
Runs distracted in the labyrinth
Of frantic trickles, trying to drop through
To sleep, to silence; steadying to music,
The metal river of the gamelan,
Gongs and bells rippling and plying
Across a thrum of water, the unhurried
Murmur of cardplay, frowsty fighting-cocks
Towsling in halfmoon wicker cages, sucking
Babies' scratchy, intercepted cries;
While we sat crowded under dripping thatch
In a small temple-compound half the night
Waiting to see the shadow-puppets; which
We never did. Obscure, unhurried, rituals
Evolved through their own logic or no-logic
Until, dazed with boredom, we gave up
Sometime in the small hours when the rain
Had slackened, and trudged out into the night,
The only Europeans there, and leaving –
Stilted, mantis-fingered, admonitory,
Took our stick-legged impatiences away

Swishing the wet sad grass.
                    Out of half-sleep
The lamp blears into life. You're there above me
In the orange skirt you wear like a sarong.
I reach my fingers up into your hair
But you begin to tell me about going
Outside somewhere. Is it that we're sleep-talking,
Or is this ordinary? And you smile
As I try to bring focus to the soft
Dream-language you are speaking; and sit up
To find you squatting on the soft brick floor,
Which is wet under you. You stare at me
Lovely and terrible, your eyes wide open
Without a notion – now I think – where in
The world you are, or what is happening.
I take you back to bed with the hurt comfort
And hungry useless-feeling love we'd wrap
Around a shaken child, frightened, dreaming.
Somehow we've got to wake and travel south.

At dawn I go and walk outside, kicking
The sand, worrying time, distance, money.
In the white soupy light a man and woman
With rucksacks on come through the bamboo gate.
They're looking for a place to stay. They're English.
(In fact they're dentists, as they tell us later,
Travelling from Australia, where they've worked
As locums, standing-in for other dentists.)
They ask where I'm from, where I'm going,
The usual questions. So I simply tell them,
I tell them, and they look at one another.
Slowly the man unstraps his pack and reaches
Elbowdeep inside, contemplatively
Rummaging. He brings out his closed fist,
Opens it to show a plastic tube.
"We've got some penicillin if you want it."

We do. You take the first dose and feel better
Within six hours. You can sit up and read
Time magazine, and eat some fruit. We talk
And lie together in the lazy hammock
Of convalescence planning where we'll go

Now that the riddling world turns right side up
Again, and we reach out so easily
To handle its uncomplicated kindness.
Riches of choice tremble with shells and sea
And the best coffee in the world. Sometime
When we're home this illness may be only
What brought you to your ideal weight again.
(And yes, let me admit it, these few years
Later, I've chosen to forget so much
Already: so much fear, so much love,
So much embarrassment, the way to wisdom
I could never accept, and cannot still.
Even those two – the intervening gods
Paying their visit under our dim thatch
That morning – did they stay or go? I can't
Remember now their faces or their names.)

Under the trees beside the beach spiders
Are lightly grappled to their webs, a span
Of legs wider than my wideopen hand;
The fisherman makes signs to you they're harmless,
Or so we think he means. He gathers up
His mended net and grins at us and goes.
After your swim you sit and watch them, poised
Tranquil over their gleaming mesh. Flawless –
Each body like a smooth blue china acorn.

And then there is the temple, on the hill
You could just climb the day before we left,
The usual cleft gate, its elaborate pillars
Matched like the twin leaves of a Rorschach blot
Through which we step, to meet only the clink clink
Of a boy kneeling carving a stone slab
Propped by a shadowed door. In the back room
We find the monk, who lives alone here. Yes,
He says, the people feed him well, and come
To talk with him and learn meditation.
The temple's been rebuilt since the last earthquake
Six years ago. He makes us tea and shows
The carved stone panels all around the building:
The life of the Buddha, pictured by ricefarmers
Whose carving is so opulent, the whorls

And loops of narrative among the branches,
The gods with their fluttery garments streaming
Between a rooftop and an ornate cloud.
But still, he says, they won't change their religion.

We sit on canvas chairs and hear the steady
Clink of the hammer echo in the garden.

                        Darkness, late autumn;
Tonight our children sleep across the landing.
Possibilities have opened, closed, opened –
You will be reading, and your hair poured out
Over your shoulders, gathering the softened light
(So I picture you, while I delay,
Questioning a lined page in a room walled with books).
Soon I shall join you, but still wait a moment
Longer to try the flavour of our luck,
And trace the other paths that might have led
Out of that place, already now imagined
More than remembered. There it is below us,
As from the plane we might perhaps have seen it
But never did – a fragment carved from memory,
An island fretted into terraces,
Its rice paddies winking like mirror-cloth,
Its trees like stone, like water, mimicking
A shadowplay we never saw, a gate
We shall climb to again one day, a hand
Hovering still to clarify some image
Out of the mass, while the resistant rock
Nudges the chisel to its native curve.